EXPERIMENTS WITH LIGHT

A TRUE BOOK

by

Salvatore Tocci

Children's Press®
A Division of Scholastic Inc.

New York Toronto London Auckland Sydney
Mexico City New Delhi Hong Kong
Danbury, Connecticut

The colorful
lights of space.

Reading Consultant
Nanci Vargus
Primary Multiage Teacher
Decatur Township Schools
Indianapolis, Indiana

Science Consultants
Robert Gardner
Former Head of Science Dept.
Salisbury Schools
Salisbury, CT

Kevin Beardmore
Former State Science
Coordinator
Indiana Dept. of Education

Library of Congress Cataloging-in-Publication Data

Tocci, Salvatore.
Experiments with light / by Salvatore Tocci.
   p.   cm.—(A True book)
   Includes bibliographical references and index.
   ISBN 0-516-22250-3 (lib. bdg.)   0-516-27349-3 (pbk.)
1.Light—Experiments—Juvenile literature. 2. Optics—Experiments—
Juvenile literature. [1. Light—Experiments. 2. Experiments.] I. Title. II.
Series.

QC360 .T63 2001
535'.078—dc1   00-052117

Contents

Nowadays, people either fish with a bait and hook or use a lure to attract fish.

Where Are the Fish?

Have you ever gone fishing? To catch fish, some people put bait on the end of a hook. Then they drop the bait in the water and wait for the fish to eat it. Other people attach small objects called lures to the end of the fishing line. Then they drop the lure, with or without bait, into the water and wait for the fish to bite it. But long ago, people simply looked in the water and waited for the fish to appear.

For example, Native Americans used to fish in shallow water with a stick that had a sharp point at the end. When they spotted a fish, they would throw the stick, or spear, into the water to catch the fish. In deeper water, Native Americans used

Before bait and lures, people had to fish with sharpened sticks.

to sit in canoes or kayaks and caught fish using bows and arrows. The arrow had a line attached to it. This way the fish could be brought back to the boat after the arrow caught the fish.

No matter how they fished, these Native Americans never aimed directly at the fish. They knew that if they did aim directly at the fish, they would never catch it. Instead, they aimed at a spot in the water just below where they saw the fish. To learn why they aimed this way, you can carry out experiments with something that you depend on everyday—light.

What Is Light?

Light is a wave that travels through space. It is like a wave of water that moves across the sea. The waves that we can see are called visible light and are only a small part of all the light waves that travel through space. You probably think of visible light as something that

The light we see is only a small part of all of the waves that travel through space (above). Computer monitors (right) give off light.

comes from the sun, a light bulb, or a fire. Televisions and computer monitors also produce light that we can see.

Light waves travel very fast through space. In fact, nothing travels faster than light. Light waves travel through space at over 186,000 miles (299,274 kilometers) every second. This

It takes light from the sun 8 minutes to reach the Earth, even though light travels at over 186,000 miles per second!

is so fast that light from the sun takes about 8 minutes to travel the 93 million miles (149,637,000 km) to Earth. If you were to drive at 60 miles per hour, it would take you 177 years to travel this same distance!

Even though light travels so fast, you can still control what it does. For one thing, you can block it. When you do this, you make a shadow. Another thing you can do is to change the direction in which light travels.

Blocking the sun creates a shadow.

All you need is something that will bounce the light waves in the direction you would like the light to go. A mirror is the easiest thing to use to bounce, or reflect, light. What else can you use to reflect light?

Reflecting Light

You will need:
- narrow glass jar with a screw-on lid
- nail, hammer
- newspaper
- masking tape
- flashlight
- shallow bucket

Use the hammer and nail to punch two holes in the lid of the jar. Fill the jar three-quarters full with water. Screw on the lid. Wrap the jar in several layers of newspaper. Use the masking tape to hold the newspaper around the jar. Hold the jar on top of the flashlight. Turn on the flashlight so that the light shines

Be careful with the hammer and nail when making two holes in the lid of the jar.

into the jar. Take the flashlight, jar, and bucket into a closet and turn off all the lights except the flashlight. Pour the water slowly from the jar into the bucket. What happens? Does the light seem to pour out of the jar like water?

Because it is reflected by the water, light also seems to pour out of the jar.

The newspaper blocks the light so that it cannot travel out of the jar. All the light must travel through the water in the jar. The water that pours out of the jar reflects the light. This water acts like a wall that keeps bouncing the light back and forth. Because the light keeps reflecting off of the water, light seems to pour out of the jar just like water. Is there anything else you can do to light besides block it and reflect it?

15

Refracting Light

You will need:
- transparent tape
- coin
- bowl

Tape the coin to the bottom of the bowl and place the bowl on a table. You can see the coin because light waves reflect off the coin and travel to your eyes. While looking at the coin, move backward slowly until you no longer see it. Why can't you see the coin? You can't see it because the bowl blocks the light waves that bounce off the coin from reaching your eyes.

Back up far enough and eventually the coin will seem to disappear.

Now, stay in this position while some-one slowly pours water into the bowl. You will again see the coin. But is the coin where you see it? Why not?

The water actually bends the light waves traveling from the coin to your eyes. This bending of light is called refraction.

Is this school of fish really where it seems to be?

Refraction occurs whenever you look at an object, like a fish, in water. Native Americans did not know about refraction. All they knew was that the fish were really not where they saw them in the water. Refraction can fool our eyes. However, it can also make us see better.

How Can We See Better?

Obviously, we see with our eyes. Our eyes are built to detect visible light waves as they travel through space. The eye contains a lens. The lens bends, or refracts, the light waves so that they are brought together on the retina in the back of the eye. Signals

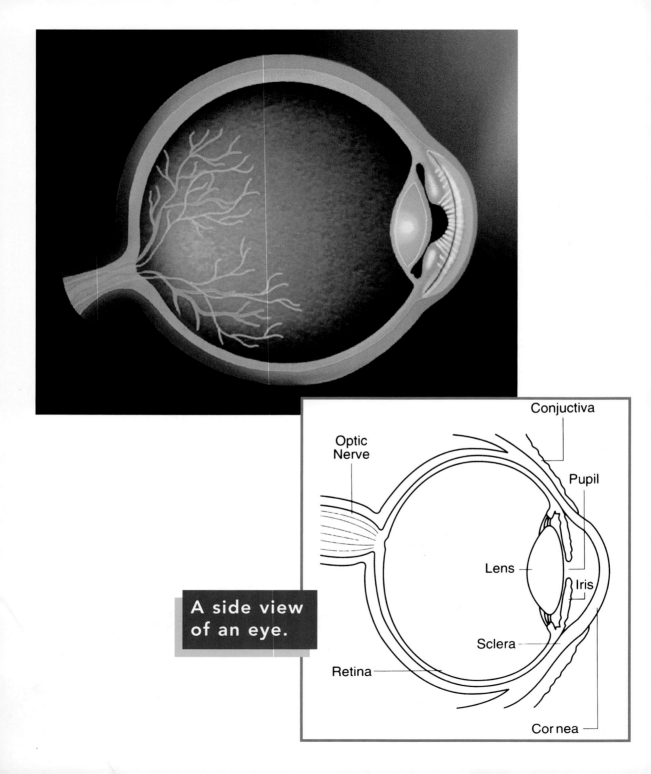

A side view of an eye.

Conjuctiva

Optic Nerve

Pupil

Lens

Iris

Sclera

Retina

Cornea

are then sent from the retina to the brain. The brain decodes these signals into images.

Sometimes the lens does not refract light correctly. When this happens, the light waves are not focused on the retina. The brain does not get the right signals, so the person cannot see as well. This problem can be fixed by wearing contact lenses or glasses. How do these work?

Focusing Light Waves

You will need:
- ruler
- pencil
- empty shoe box (no lid)
- scissors
- sheet of white paper
- small glass jar
- flashlight

Use the ruler to draw two straight vertical lines about one inch (2.54 centimeters) apart on one end of the shoe box. Cut along each line to make a narrow slit. Cut the sheet of white paper so that it covers the bottom of the shoe box.

Cut along the lines to make a narrow slit.

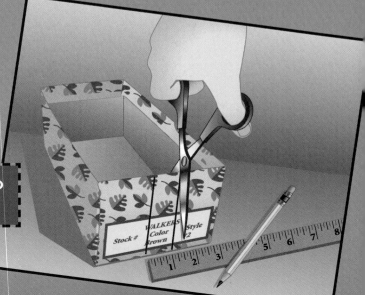

Fill the jar with water. Place the jar in the middle of the box and line it up with the two slits. Darken the room. Shine the flashlight through the two slits.

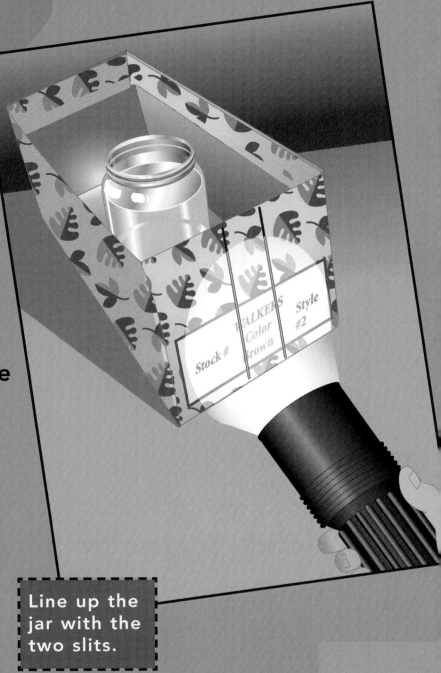

Line up the jar with the two slits.

Notice what happens to the light waves as they pass through the glass. The glass refracts the light waves so that they come together at a point.

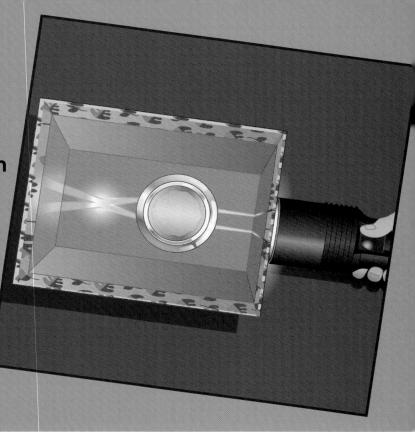

Both contact lenses and eye glasses refract light waves so that they are focused correctly on the retina. How else can lenses help us see better?

Magnifying Images

Use the scissors to punch out three round holes around the side of the tube near its bottom. Put one of the objects you want to look at on the table. Place the tube around the object. Cover the top of the tube with plastic wrap. Gently push down on the plastic wrap to make a small depression in the center. Use the rubber band to hold the plastic wrap in place. Slowly pour some water into the depression.

Now, look down into the tube. Does the object look bigger? The water and the plastic wrap act like a magnifying lens. They refract light coming from the objects,

View of a button with and without magnification by the water and plastic wrap.

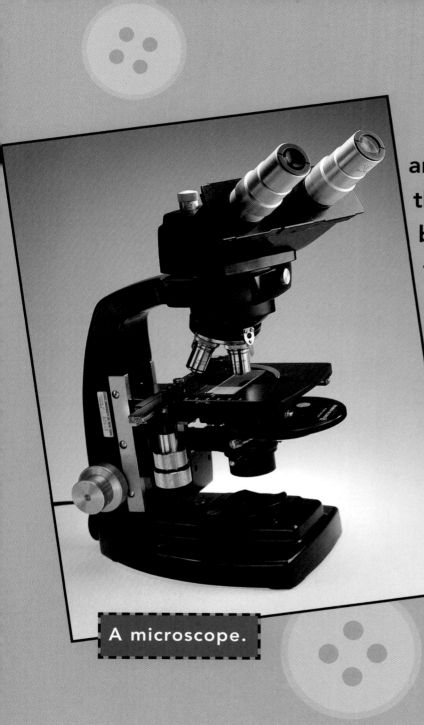

and they make the objects look bigger. Lenses that magnify images are used in microscopes. What else can lenses do besides focus and magnify?

A microscope.

Seeing Objects Up Close

You will need:
- a small, curved mirror like one used for putting on cosmetics
- a small, flat mirror
- magnifying lens

Hold the curved mirror by a window so that it points to an object outside, like a tree. Ask someone to hold the small, flat mirror so that you can see a reflection of the curved mirror in the middle. Hold the magnifying lens and look at the reflection in the flat mirror.

Magnifying lenses make things appear much closer than they actually are.

The object will appear much closer than when you look at it with just your eyes.

A telescope.

What you have made is a simple telescope. Telescopes make things look closer than they really are. Some telescopes, like the one you made, use mirrors to reflect light. The reflection of light also helps us see a world that is full of colors.

Where Do Colors Come From?

Light from the sun or a light bulb appears colorless. We call this light "white light." White light, however, is really a mixture of several different colors. You can show this by passing white light through certain materials, such as a prism. What you

Prisms produce a rainbow of colors.

see is a rainbow of colors. Is there another way to split white light into different colors?

Making a Rainbow

You will need:
- masking tape
- baking pan
- flat mirror
- white cardboard
- sunlight

Put some tape along the bottom of the baking pan near one edge. Fill the bottom of the pan with water and set it near a window. Rest the mirror on the tape so that it leans against the side of the pan. Move the pan so that sunlight shines on the mirror. Hold a piece of white cardboard in front of the mirror. What colors do you see?

The water acts as a prism that splits sunlight into the different colors. This same thing happens when you see a rainbow in the sky. Droplets of water in the air can split the light when the sun begins to shine again. If you can split white light to make different colors, what happens if you mix different colors?

Rainbows are light divided into colors.

Experiment 7

💡

Mixing Colors

You will need:
- transparent tape
- red, blue, and green cellophane
- 3 flashlights
- white paper

Tape a piece of different color cellophane over the bulb end of each flashlight. Tape the white paper to a wall. Darken the room. Shine the red and green flashlights on the white paper. Move the lights so that they overlap. What color do you see? Mixing red and green makes yellow. Mix the blue and green lights, and you should get a color called cyan. What happens when you mix the blue and red lights? You should get the color magenta.

Combining blue and red creates magenta.

You made yellow by mixing red and green lights. Then does this mean that something is yellow because it is being struck by red and green lights? No, this is not why objects are yellow. The following experiment will show you why an object has a certain color, such as yellow.

Seeing Colors

You will need:
- lamp
- red cellophane
- tape
- plant with leaves

Cover the bulb in the lamp with red cellophane. Tape the cellophane in place so that the whole bulb stays covered. Put the lamp near a plant. Darken the room and turn on the lamp. What color are the leaves?

In the sun or in the light from a bulb, a leaf is struck by

The leaf absorbs the colors that strike it.

all the colors you see in a rainbow. The leaf absorbs, or holds on to, most of these colors. The only color the leaf reflects is green, so it looks green. The color of any object depends on the color of light that the object reflects. For example, a blue shirt absorbs every color except blue. The shirt reflects blue light, so it looks blue.

This shirt looks blue because it absorbs every color of light except for blue.

But why does a green leaf look black in red light? Remember that a leaf looks green because the only color it reflects is green light. When you put a leaf in red light, there is no green light for it to reflect. If the leaf does not reflect any light at all, then it looks black.

You have learned that light travels as waves through space. When light waves strike something, like a mirror or water, they can be either bounced back or bent. Light waves can be bent so much that an object under water, like a fish, is not really where it seems to be.

Fun With Light

Now that you've learned a few things about light, here's a fun experiment to do. See how light can trick your brain into thinking that you have a hole in your hand.

Playing a Trick

You will need:
- piece of paper
- tape

Roll up the paper. Tape it to make a long tube. Keeping both eyes open, look through the tube with your right eye. Hold up your left hand next to the tube with your palm toward you and rest your pinky along the edge of the tube.

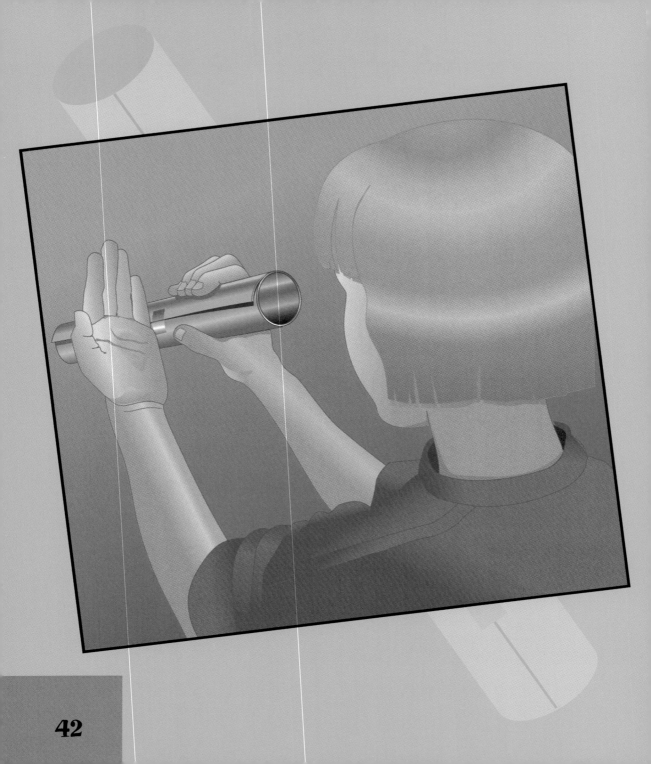

Keep both eyes open. Slowly move your palm toward your nose along the tube. You should see that part of your palm is missing!

Obviously you are not missing anything. Light is simply playing a trick on your brain. Your right eye sees inside the tube. This appears as a hole to your brain. Your left eye sees your palm. The brain is getting two different signals, so it combines the two. What you see then is a hole, or a piece missing in your palm. This is an example of an optical illusion.

To Find Out More

If you would like to learn more about light, check out these additional resources.

Books

Dixon, Malcolm, and Karen Smith. **Light and Color.** Smart Apple Media, 1999.

Gardner, Robert. **Experiments with Light and Mirrors.** Enslow Publishing, 1995.

Jennings, Terry. **Light.** Raintree Steck-Vaughn, 1994.

Murray, Peter. **Light Science Tricks.** The Child's World, 1998.

Nankivell-Aston, Sally, and Dorothy Jackson. **Science Experiments with Light.** Franklin Watts, 2000.

The Exploratorium
3601 Lyon Street
San Francisco, CA 94123
415-397-5673

Check out their Science Explorer site at *http://www.exploratorium. edu/science_explorer/index. html.* You will find several experiments you can do under "Seeing the Light," including how to make a camera from a potato chip can.

National Aeronautics and Space Administration (NASA)
Log on to NASA's site at *http://www.thegateway.org/ simplesearch.html.* Enter the search word "light" and click on your grade level. You will then be given a list of sites that you can explore for more information about light.

Optics for Kids
http://www.opticalres.com/ kidoptx.html

This site has more information about lenses, including lenses that are used in cameras. You can also learn about a special kind of light called a laser light.

Important Words

absorb take in

lens part of the eye; also glass that is
made to refract light

light wave that travels through space

optical illusion trick played on our
eyes by light

prism glass that can split light into
colors

reflect bounce back

refract bend

retina back of the eye where light is
focused

visible light light we can see

white light light made by mixing all
the colors of light we see

Index

Meet the Author

Salvatore Tocci is a science writer who lives in East Hampton, New York, with his wife Patti. He was a high school biology and chemistry teacher for almost 30 years. As a teacher, he always encouraged his students to do experiments to learn about science. When he is not writing, he loves to spend time in his darkroom using light to develop black-and-white photographs. His photographs have appeared in both newspapers and books.

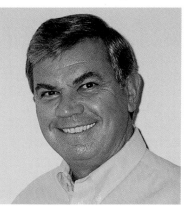